# REFORMING WELFARE
# WITH WORK

# REFORMING WELFARE WITH WORK

## by Judith M. Gueron*

Occasional Paper Number Two
Ford Foundation Project on
Social Welfare and the American Future

* Judith M. Gueron is president of Manpower
Demonstration Research Corporation, New York.

One of a series of reports on activities supported by the Ford Foundation. A complete list of publications may be obtained from the Ford Foundation, Office of Reports, 320 East 43 Street, New York, New York 10017.

**Library of Congress Cataloging-in-Publication Data**

Gueron, Judith M.
  Reforming welfare with work.

  (Occasional paper / Ford Foundation Project on Social Welfare and the American Future; no. 2)
    Includes bibliographical references.
    1. Public welfare—Government policy—United States.
I. Title. II. Series.
HV95.G84 1987          361.6′14′0973          87-23595
ISBN 0-916584-30-5

## EXECUTIVE PANEL
### Ford Foundation Project on Social Welfare and the American Future

# Contents

# Foreword

The United States has a two-pronged system of social welfare—one that is designed for labor-force participants and the other for those who do not work. For workers, a combination of employee benefit and government social insurance programs provides protection against the risks of illness, disability, and unemployment and also sets aside funds for income maintenance and health coverage during the retirement years. Nonworkers, mainly children, the disabled, and the elderly, are sustained by a governmental safety net program. Except for low-income single parents with young children, able-bodied, working-age adults are expected to work and thereby provide for their needs.

Does this social welfare system, designed in large part in the 1930s, provide sufficient protection for Americans as they are about to enter the 21st century? Have significant holes developed in the fabric of social protection, and, if so, is society willing to pay for mending them? Has the changing composition of the U.S. population, specifically the increase in the elderly and single-parent families, altered the premises on which the system was built? Why is there such a persistently high level of poverty, in good times and bad, and can anything be done to correct it? Can more be done to help the troubling number of American children who experience at least some poverty in their growing-up years?

These are some of the questions that the Ford Foundation set out to answer when in 1985 it launched a wide-ranging inquiry into alternative approaches to providing social insurance and welfare services, taking into account changes in the economy, in the family and work, and in the nation's age profile. Called the Project on Social Welfare and the American Future, the inquiry is led by a twelve-member executive panel of citizens representing the business, academic, civil rights, and labor communities.* Chairman of the panel is Irving S. Shapiro, until recently a member of the Foundation's Board of Trustees and a former chief executive officer of the du Pont Company.

In the course of its inquiry, the panel has commissioned a number of research reports and convened sessions of social policy experts to discuss approaches to such interrelated topics as health care, retirement and pension policy, poverty and welfare policy, and public and private social welfare programs. For one of the sessions, in November 1986, the panel invited leading scholars and practitioners in the field of poverty and welfare to discuss the policy implications of their work. They were asked to address three topics: the diverse and interrelated causes of poverty, the consequences of poverty for individuals and society as a whole, and whether the safety net and training programs developed since the 1930s are appropriate for fighting poverty in the 1980s and beyond.

Together with several specially commissioned research reports, the papers offer an unusually comprehensive picture of why people are poor and what has been and might be done about it. For this reason, the Foundation has decided to publish them, beginning with David Ellwood's review of our various income-maintenance programs and Judith Gueron's paper on how the welfare system might be reformed. Other papers will follow. They include discussions of the current social protection system and its shortcomings; of the macroeconomic, behavioral, and human capital explanations

---

* Members of the panel are listed on page *v.*

for poverty; of the potential of new management approaches to improve the efficiency of government social programs; and the role of health care, child support, education, training, and tax incentives in reducing different kinds of poverty. The views expressed in the papers are the authors' own and do not necessarily reflect those of members of the executive panel or of the staff and board of the Ford Foundation.

We are grateful to the authors for taking time out from their busy schedules to set down their thoughts on a complex range of issues. Together they have made a useful contribution to the current debate over social welfare policy.

**Franklin A. Thomas**
**President**
**Ford Foundation**

# Introduction

This country has long debated the question of how to design the welfare system—particularly the federally supported Aid to Families with Dependent Children (AFDC) program, which provides cash assistance to families headed primarily by female single parents. The debate has intensified as welfare reform once again has become a presidential priority. A pressing issue before Congress is whether welfare programs should continue to be broad entitlements or whether, instead, they should become "reciprocal obligations," whereby work—or participation in an activity leading to work—is required in return for public aid. Although other features of welfare reform have been aired recently, they have not yet been thoroughly discussed or studied.

Fortunately, the body of knowledge on work approaches has grown considerably during the last five years. In 1982 the Manpower Demonstration Research Corporation (MDRC) began a five-year study examining eight state initiatives that attempt to restructure the relationship between welfare and work. The evaluations in five states have been completed.[1]

This paper first sets the context for the discussion by outlining the issues surrounding the AFDC program and the evolution of the debate about reforming welfare with work. It then summarizes the major findings of the MDRC study. In conclusion, it suggests some of the implications of these findings for welfare policy and discusses important unanswered questions.[2]

1

# Background:
# The AFDC Program and the
# Pressure for Reform

The current AFDC program is one way of balancing the competing values and objectives of social welfare policy: to reduce poverty (especially among children), to promote family stability, to encourage mothers and fathers to support themselves and their families, and to minimize costs. Today's debate about the program echoes a central dilemma that was identified as long ago as the English Poor Laws: Is it possible to assist the poor without, by that very act, giving people incentives for behavior that perpetuates poverty and dependency? This question, in turn, rests on ideas about who the poor are and what has caused their condition.

Although the debate about AFDC has long recognized that the multiple objectives of the program cannot all be maximized and that any welfare system involves trade-offs, at issue is whether the existing AFDC program represents the best balance possible, given current values and knowledge.

Of particular concern in AFDC policy are questions about whether it reduces the incentives for people to work and whether it promotes a "culture of poverty" (for example, teenage pregnancy and multigenerational dependency). The arguments are simple:

- Most people have to work for income. Welfare recipients have an alternative.

3

- In addition, the very rules of AFDC and all other income-conditioned programs serve to "tax" the income gained by people who do work: these rates are often very high. As a result, the structure of the AFDC program makes work less attractive and encourages dependency.
- Although AFDC has been criticized for not providing sufficient income, any attempt to increase welfare grants to levels that provide a decent standard of living for adults and children will only increase the disincentives for recipients to take low-paying jobs.
- Since AFDC eligibility is open primarily to women heading households and since benefits depend on the number of children, the very design of the program may discourage family formation and allow fathers to avoid supporting their children.

Unfortunately, it is easier to describe the arguments than to quantify the extent to which poverty or female-headed families actually result from welfare programs rather than from other social or economic forces.

It is also difficult to devise alternative policies that perform better. There are a number of reasons why reform has proven elusive. First, the debate surrounding the appropriate policy connection between work and welfare has frequently been highly charged, dealing as it does with central issues of income redistribution, social justice, and individual responsibility. Since there is no consensus on the relative importance of the different policy objectives, efforts at reform that succeed better in meeting one objective—but only at the expense of reducing another—usually encounter strong opposition. Second, the lack of reliable data on the alleged negative effects of welfare makes it difficult to assess the actual trade-offs involved in different reform options.

There is also persistent disagreement on the causes of poverty and welfare dependency, with different diagnoses suggesting different cures. Some blame the disincentives embodied in welfare programs themselves, while others stress the limited education, skills, and work experience of the poor. Some highlight health problems or negative attitudes toward work, and still others point to the labor market, with its lack of opportunities for employment and advancement. The importance of these non-welfare factors suggests that changing the AFDC rules will be only one step in any attack on poverty.

In the past twenty-five years, three basic approaches have been taken to reform welfare in order to better reconcile the central values listed above. The first would change the rules for determining welfare eligibility and the size of benefits in order to increase the financial incentives for choosing work instead of welfare (that is, it would encourage recipients to increase their work effort voluntarily). The second would transform the AFDC entitlement into a "bargain," in which an AFDC grant carries with it some reciprocal obligation to accept a job, to search for work, or to participate in work experience, education, or training activities in preparation for work. This second approach has been mandatory, in that an individual can lose AFDC benefits for failing to cooperate with the program requirements. A third strategy has been to rely less on AFDC cash grants and more on alternatives that provide other incentives: for example, child-support enforcement, changes in tax policy that increase the rewards for work, and the direct provision of training or jobs.

The discussion below outlines why the welfare reform debate has increasingly shifted toward the second approach— work solutions—and presents the evidence on the feasibility and effectiveness of this strategy. (Throughout, this paper focuses on welfare programs directed to families, not to the aged or disabled.)

## The AFDC Program

Public assistance programs in the United States have tried to make sharp distinctions between those considered able to work and those judged appropriate for public support. Working-age men have been included in the former category—and they have received only limited support in the welfare system. The aged and severely disabled are classified in the latter category. There has been more controversy about poor single mothers, with a recent major shift in the relative emphasis given to ensuring the well-being of children and encouraging their parents to support themselves by working.

When the AFDC program was adopted as part of the Social Security Act of 1935, it was regarded primarily as a means to provide assistance to poor children. The initial assumption was that only a small group of poor mothers would receive benefits on behalf of their children: widows and the wives of disabled workers who—like other women—should have the opportunity to stay at home and care for their children. The issue of work incentives did not arise since these were cases of hardship, not choice. The focus was on child welfare, and encouraging mothers to enter the work force was not seen as a route toward that goal.

In recent years, several factors have led to a change in public perceptions about the appropriateness of employment for welfare mothers— including mothers of very young children.

First, in the 1960s and early 1970s AFDC caseloads and costs grew rapidly, as did the proportion of the caseload headed by women who were divorced or never married. Second, the employment rates of all women— including single parents and women with very young children—increased dramatically, leading many to reconsider the equity and appropriateness of supporting welfare mothers who could be working. Third, although recent research confirms that most people use welfare only for short-term support, it also points to a not insignificant group for whom AFDC serves as a source of long-term assistance. The growing concern about the presumed negative effects of such dependency on adults and children has prompted intensified efforts to reach this group.

All of these developments have raised questions about whether the design of the AFDC program is not part of the problem.

## Strategies for Reforming AFDC

All AFDC reform efforts have grappled with the challenge of providing adequate income while maintaining incentives for work and self-sufficiency, and doing both at a reasonable cost. Years of debate have confirmed the impossibility of simultaneously maximizing all of these objectives and have also identified some of the trade-offs that the different approaches imply.

During the period from the mid-1960s to the early 1970s, many attempts to increase the employment of welfare recipients centered on building financial incentives for work into the AFDC program itself. As a first step, the 1967 amendments to the Social Security Act reduced the rate at which welfare grants decreased (the implicit marginal "tax" rate) when recipients went to work.

Then interest shifted and the debate centered on the advantages of replacing AFDC with a universal, noncategorical, negative income tax. This was proposed in the Nixon Administration's Family Assistance Plan, which would have guaranteed a minimum income to all Americans, not only single-parent families but also the working poor. It was hoped that this expanded coverage would lessen the incentives for family dissolution and, at the same time, would not seriously reduce work effort. However, some have argued that the findings from several of the federally sponsored income-maintenance experiments suggest that more generous financial incentives to work would have increased the size of the beneficiary population and actually reduced, rather than increased, overall work effort.[3] For many people, this new evidence eliminated the possibility of welfare reform by means of a comprehensive negative income tax system.

As a result, the welfare reform proposals of both the Carter and Reagan administrations have included some form of a comprehensive work obligation, under which "employable" welfare recipients would have to accept a job or participate in a work-related activity. These plans relied on mandatory requirements to provide an incentive—through the threat of a loss of welfare benefits—for welfare recipients to work.

An early harbinger of this policy shift was the enactment of the Work Incentive (WIN) Program. Introduced as a discretionary program in 1967, WIN became mandatory in 1971; that is, in order to receive AFDC benefits, all adult recipients without preschool children or specific problems that kept them at home would have to register with the state employment service, to participate in job training or job-search activities, and to accept employment offers. In theory WIN imposed a participation obligation, but the program was never funded at a level adequate to create the precondition for a real work test: a "slot" for each able-bodied person.

Under pressure to increase the work effort and reduce the AFDC rolls, both the Carter and the 1981 Reagan proposals called for a redefinition of the welfare entitlement. The two designs had striking similarities that are usually overlooked. Both suggested that the right to welfare benefits be linked with an obligation to work: that is, employable AFDC recipients who failed to locate jobs would be required to work as a condition of receiving public aid.

There were, however, important differences in the amount and the form of that aid. The Carter proposal guaranteed welfare recipients full-time public service employment (PSE) jobs and paid them wages. In contrast, the Reagan Administration's universal "workfare" plan mandated that recipients work in exchange for their welfare grants, with no compensation beyond the public assistance check (except for the limited reimbursement of working expenses). In all states except those with the highest grants, the workfare formulation would lead to part-time work and continued low income.[4] (Here and elsewhere in this paper, the word "workfare" is used to describe a mandatory work-for-benefits program, and not the evolving broader definition that encompasses any form of work-related obligation or option.)

The special appeal of restating the AFDC "bargain" this way lies in its seeming to reconcile the conflicting welfare policy objectives, at the same time as it may provide a direct attack on the causes of poverty and dependency. The claimed advantages of this approach include:

- *Strengthening work incentives and bringing AFDC into line with prevailing values.* By design, such programs provide the strongest work incentives, since benefits are conditioned on meeting a work requirement. Welfare recipients would have an obligation that parallels the one faced by other citizens and that fits with mainstream American values and the belief in the work ethic—values shared by the general public and by welfare recipients.
- *Improving the employability of welfare recipients.* It was hoped that work programs would increase human capital, indirectly by instilling a sense of responsibility or the work ethic, and directly by developing skills by means of well-structured work experience. To ensure that this occurred, some states have extended the range of mandatory activities to include education and training.
- *Providing social benefits.* To the extent that workfare and public service employment strategies create additional positions and meaningful work, they also promise to provide useful public services.
- *Reducing the welfare rolls.* Mandatory work approaches, it was hoped, would reduce welfare dependency by deterrence and assistance. Because of the new requirements, some individuals might not apply for welfare and others might leave the rolls more quickly. Some might refuse work assignments because of conflicts with unreported jobs and then be "sanctioned;" i.e., removed from the rolls. Others, benefiting from new skills or from a work record, might find it easier to obtain unsubsidized jobs.
- *Psychological benefits and public support.* Supporters also have argued that forging a direct connection between welfare and work bestows greater dignity on recipients, has positive effects on the worker and his or her family, and increases public support for the AFDC program.

Critics challenged the ability of both the Carter and Reagan proposals to satisfy these claims. Given the existing service delivery system and the nature of the welfare population, they questioned whether a large-scale participation and work requirement could be enforced in a manner that met acceptable standards of fairness. For example, how would these programs differentiate between recipients who should be excused from any obligation for good cause, and those who should be penalized for noncompliance? This dilemma was particularly challenging, given the widespread recognition that there was no easy and straightforward formula to determine the "employability" of female household heads, which would depend on diverse and changing factors such as health and the availability of child care.[5] Many also questioned whether a sufficient number of useful jobs could be created that would provide employment skills and yet not displace regular workers, and, if not, whether jobs for welfare recipients would become punitive or "make-work."

Critics also thought that workfare or public service employment would not speed the transition to unsubsidized work because the economy did not generate enough regular jobs, and program services were of limited value in helping recipients obtain available ones. Moreover, some questioned the assumption that people would move off the rolls to avoid a work obligation, seeing no need to create a work ethic that was already there. As a result, they argued that the additional costs of administering a work program would exceed any potential welfare savings. Finally, critics maintained that public employees and other groups would not accept the supplementation of the work force by unpaid or low-paid public assistance recipients.

Although many of these criticisms were directed both at the Carter and the Reagan proposals, welfare advocates for the most part preferred the Carter public service employment approach to the Reagan workfare model. In addition, advocates favored expanding the list of required activities to include education and training and wanted to increase the level of support services. Such measures appeared to shift the balance away from obligation toward opportunity.

Ultimately, the high cost of the Carter Administration's proposal— the Congressional Budget Office put a price tag of more than $15 billion a year on the Program for Better Jobs and Income—led to its rejection. The Reagan Administration's 1981 version was treated more favorably. Although Congress did not mandate a national program, the states could choose to implement workfare. The states that did so have often made further changes that have transformed it from a straight work requirement—in which recipients "pay back" society—to one that aims as much to assist people in leaving welfare as to have them fulfill an obligation while they are on welfare.

# Lessons from the 1980s: An Evaluation of State Work/Welfare Initiatives

In passing the Omnibus Budget Reconciliation Act of 1981 (OBRA), Congress reflected a growing consensus on the need for welfare recipients to work and to become more self-supporting and, at the same time, uncertainty about the feasibility and effectiveness of the proposal for universal workfare. The legislation gave states a chance to experiment, albeit within the context of sharply reduced funding.

The Community Work Experience Program (CWEP), a provision of OBRA, made it possible for the first time for states to choose to make workfare mandatory for AFDC recipients. States also were authorized to fund on-the-job training programs by using a recipient's welfare grant as a wage subsidy for private employers. In addition, primarily through a new option known as the WIN Demonstration Program, they could change the institutional arrangements for delivering employment and training services and were allowed greater flexibility in the mix of these services. In many states, the OBRA possibilities seemed to trigger a new resolve on the part of state administrators to make WIN participation requirements more meaningful than they had been in the past.

In 1982, the Manpower Demonstration Research Corporation began a five-year social experiment to examine the new state work initiatives. MDRC's Demonstration of State Work/Welfare Initiatives is a series of large-scale evaluations in eight states and smaller-scale studies in three additional

13

states. Major funding for the study was provided by the Ford Foundation, matched by grants from other private foundations and the participating states, which, in general, received no special operating funds.

As a result, the project is not a test of centrally developed and funded reform proposals, but of programs designed at the state level in the new environment of OBRA flexibility and constrained funding. And, because these initiatives are often the state's WIN Demonstration Program, the study for the first time provides rigorous answers on the effectiveness of the WIN Program in its 1980s WIN Demonstration incarnation.[6]

To ensure that the project produced findings of national relevance, the states selected are broadly representative of national variations in local conditions, administrative arrangements, and AFDC benefit levels— which, for a family of three in 1982 in the participating states ranged from a low of $140 per month in Arkansas to a high of $526 in California. Demonstration locations include all or part of several large urban areas—San Diego, Baltimore, and Chicago—and a number of large multicounty areas spanning both urban and rural centers in the states of Arkansas, Maine, New Jersey, Virginia, and West Virginia. (Table 1, on pages 16 and 17, summarizes the key features of the eight state programs and the different groups studied in each state.[7])

The study tests not one program model but a range of strategies, reflecting differences in state philosophies, objectives, and funding. Some states have limited their programs to one or two activities; others offer a wider mix. A few programs are voluntary, but most require participation as a condition of receiving welfare benefits.

In designing their programs, many states chose job-search activities and unpaid work experience. The job-search strategy is based on the assumption that many welfare recipients are currently employable but have not found jobs because they do not know how (or are not sufficiently motivated) to look for them. Job search does not train people for specific jobs but encourages and teaches them how to seek employment.

Two versions of mandatory unpaid work experience exist in six of the states. In the first, the CWEP or workfare version, work hours are determined by dividing the AFDC grant by the minimum wage. The work requirements can be either limited in duration or ongoing—that is, they last as long as the recipients remain on welfare. In the second version— usually called WIN Work Experience because it was first used in the national WIN Program—the number of hours worked is unrelated to the grant level and participation is generally limited to thirteen weeks.

Contrary to some expectations, the states in the study— reflecting the larger national response to OBRA—did not choose to implement universal workfare. Mandatory job search was more widely used. Among the demonstration states, only West Virginia (with its unusual labor market conditions) followed the model originally offered to the states as an option in the 1981 legislation: workfare with no limit on the length of a recipient's participation. The West Virginia program, however, was directed primarily to men receiving assistance under the AFDC program for unemployed heads of two-parent families (AFDC-U). The state placed less emphasis on workfare for women receiving AFDC.

Other programs (in Arkansas, San Diego, and Chicago) established a two-stage sequence consisting of job search followed by a work obligation (usually limited to thirteen weeks) for those who had not found unsubsidized jobs in the first phase. Virginia required job search of everyone and offered short-term workfare as a later option among other mandatory services. Baltimore operated a range of educational and training services (including job search and unpaid work experience), with participants' choices tailored to their needs and preferences. Two states—New Jersey and Maine— implemented voluntary on-the-job training programs with private employers, using the diversion of welfare grants as the funding mechanism.

The programs varied in scale. Although most were large, none covered the full AFDC caseload. Five operated in only part of the state. Most were targeted to women with school-

**Table 1**

Key Characteristics of State Work/Welfare Initiatives

| State/City(a) | Program Model and Nature of Requirement to Participate(b) | Study Area(c) | Target Group |
|---|---|---|---|
| Arkansas | Mandatory program. Job-search workshop followed by individual job search and 12 weeks of work experience in public and private nonprofit agencies. | Pulaski South and Jefferson Counties | WIN-mandatory AFDC applicants and recipients including women with children aged 3 to 5. |
| San Diego, California | Mandatory program. Job-search workshop followed by 13 weeks of CWEP in public and private nonprofit agencies. | County-wide | WIN-mandatory AFDC and AFDC-U applicants. |
| Chicago, Illinois | Mandatory program. Individual job search followed by activities, including 13 weeks of work experience. | Cook County | WIN-mandatory AFDC applicants and recipients (including recently approved cases). |

| | | | |
|---|---|---|---|
| Maine | Voluntary program. Pre-vocational training, 12 weeks of work experience and on-the-job training funded by grant diversion. | Statewide | AFDC recipients on welfare for at least six consecutive months. |
| Baltimore, Maryland | Mandatory program. Multicomponent including job search, education, training, on-the-job training, and 13 weeks of work experience. | 10 out of 18 Income-Maintenance Centers | WIN-mandatory AFDC and AFDC-U applicants and recipients. |
| New Jersey | Voluntary program. On-the-job training funded by grant diversion. | 9 of 21 counties | WIN-mandatory and voluntary AFDC recipients. |
| Virginia | Mandatory program. Job search followed by 13 weeks of CWEP, education, or training. | 11 of 124 agencies (4 urban, 7 rural) | WIN-mandatory AFDC applicants and recipients. |
| West Virginia | Mandatory program. CWEP—unlimited duration—in public and private nonprofit agencies. | 9 of 27 administrative areas | WIN-mandatory AFDC and AFDC-U applicants and recipients. |

*Notes:*

(a) In Arkansas and Maryland, a full evaluation was conducted in the indicated counties and a process study was done in other counties.

(b) In San Diego, Chicago, and Virginia there were two different experimental treatments.

(c) In addition to the study areas, Virginia and West Virginia implemented the program statewide and Arkansas, Illinois, and Maryland in selected other areas.

age children—the only group traditionally required to register with WIN—who typically represent about one-third of the adults heading AFDC cases. Some worked only with subsets of this mandatory group—for example, people who had recently applied for welfare and were new to the rolls—while others included both new applicants and those who were already welfare recipients. In addition, three programs required people receiving welfare through the AFDC-U program to participate.

The states also had different objectives. Some placed relatively more emphasis on developing human capital and helping welfare recipients obtain better jobs and long-term self-sufficiency. Others stressed immediate job placement and welfare savings. The states also varied in the extent to which they emphasized and enforced a participation requirement. Although most planned to increase participation above the levels achieved in WIN, few clearly articulated a goal of full or universal participation.

## Interim Findings from the State Work Initiatives

The MDRC study is structured as a series of three-year evaluations in each state. Because the research activities were phased in at different times, the study extends over five years. Final results are now available from five of the programs—those in Arkansas, San Diego, Virginia, West Virginia, and Baltimore—and partial results are available from most of the others.[8]

The study addresses three basic questions. Each is discussed below, with the focus on overarching lessons, not on the full range of program-specific findings.

*Is it feasible to impose obligations—or participation requirements—as a condition of welfare receipt?* Pre-1981 welfare employment programs—both the WIN Program and several special demonstration programs—were generally unable to establish meaningful work-related obligations for recipients. A major question at the outset of the MDRC study was whether the existing bureaucracies would have greater success.

In some cases, the answer is "yes." In most of the states studied, participation rates are running above those in previous special demonstrations or in the WIN Program. Typically, within six to nine months of registering with the new program, about half of the AFDC group had taken part in some activity, and substantial additional numbers had left the welfare rolls and the program. Thus, for example, within nine months of welfare application in San Diego, all but a small proportion— 9 percent of the AFDC and 6 percent of the AFDC-U applicants—had either left welfare, become employed, were no longer in the program, or had fulfilled all of the program requirements. In some of the other states, the proportion of those still eligible and not reached by the program was as high as 25 percent, indicating a somewhat looser enforcement of the participation requirement. Overall, this represents a major management achievement and reflects a change in institutions and staff attitudes.

However, given the financial constraints under which states have been operating, one should not exaggerate the level of the services recipients have received or the intensity or scope of their participation obligation. By far the major activity has been job search, a relatively short-term and modest intervention. Education and training activities have been limited, and workfare, when it was required, has almost always been a short-term obligation—usually lasting thirteen weeks.

In part, this response reflects limited funds. The programs were relatively inexpensive, with average costs per enrollee ranging from $165 in Arkansas to $1,050 in Maryland. Had the typical obligation been longer or more intensive, it would have been necessary to raise the level of the initial investments in services. States have thus far managed to deliver services with generally modest funding. However, if resources remain low or are further depleted—or if the programs expand in scale—there is a risk of returning to the pre-1981 WIN approach of formal registration requirements and little real programmatic content.

*What do workfare programs look like in practice, and how do welfare recipients view the mandatory work requirements?*

Much of the workfare debate hinges on the nature of the worksite experience: that is, whether the positions are of a punitive and "make-work" nature or whether they produce useful goods and services, provide dignity, and develop work skills. MDRC addressed these questions by means of in-depth interviews with random samples of workfare supervisors and participants in six states. Results suggest that:

• The jobs were generally entry-level positions in maintenance, clerical work, park service, or human services.
• Although the positions did not primarily develop skills, they were not make-work either. Supervisors judged the work important and indicated that participants' productivity and attendance were similar to those of most entry-level workers.
• A large proportion of the participants responded positively to the work assignments. They were satisfied with the positions and with coming to work, and they believed they were making a useful contribution.
• Many participants nevertheless believed that the employer got the better end of the bargain, or that they were underpaid for their work. In brief, they would have preferred a paid job.

These findings suggest that most states did not design or implement workfare with a punitive intent. This may explain results from the worksite survey that indicated that the majority of the participants in most states shared the view that a work requirement was fair.[9] These results are consistent with findings from other studies that show that the poor want to work and are eager to take advantage of opportunities to do so. As one of MDRC's field researchers observed: these workfare programs did not create the work ethic, they found it.

Although this evidence is striking, it should not be used to draw conclusions about the quality of the programs or about the reactions of welfare recipients should workfare requirements be implemented on a larger scale, be differently designed, or last longer than the typical thirteen-week assignment in the states studied.

*Do these initiatives make a difference? Do they reduce the welfare rolls and costs and/or increase employment and earnings? How do the programs' benefits compare to their costs?* Experience suggests that these are very difficult questions to answer. Prior research shows that, contrary to popular conceptions, half of all welfare recipients normally move off the rolls—often to a job—within two years.[10] Thus, if a study points to the achievements or cost savings of a program based only on the performance of its participants—for example, based on job placements—it will overstate the program's accomplishments by taking credit for those who would have found jobs on their own. The challenge in assessing program achievements, or "impacts," is to distinguish between program-induced changes and the normal dynamics of welfare turnover and labor market behavior of this population. Accurate assessment requires data on what people would have done in the absence of the program: that is, data describing the behavior of a control group.

In eight of the states in MDRC's study, the research is structured to meet the major objection leveled at many earlier evaluations: that their control groups did not correctly mimic the behavior of the participants or that they had no control group at all. The human resources commissioners in these eight states acted with notable foresight. In an unusual display of commitment to high standards of program evaluation, they cooperated with the random assignment of more than 35,000 individuals to different groups, with some participating in the program (or several program variations) and some placed in a control group, receiving limited or no program services.

It is very rare to be able to conduct an evaluation with this degree of reliability. In fact, never before has a major part of the nation's employment and training system been assessed on this scale, using an "experimental" methodology based on random assignment. Typically, researchers have had to contend with studies that yield a great deal of data but produce little evidence about what the program has actually accomplished. Often, "results" merely show what would have happened to participants in the normal course of events. In contrast, a study using random assignment sets a demanding standard for what can be registered as change and accurately pinpoints the real achievements of the program.

Assessing the impact and the benefit-cost results to date is very much like looking at a glass and characterizing it as half full or half empty. Depending on one's perspective, there are real accomplishments or there is a basis for caution. In either case, the findings are complex and require a careful reading. The balance of this section presents the positive view and then discusses potential limitations on what the programs can achieve.

First, the results dispel the notion that employment and training interventions do not work. In light of the findings for these work/welfare initiatives, it is no longer defensible to argue that welfare employment initiatives have no value. Using a variety of approaches, four of the five programs studied thus far produced positive employment gains for AFDC women. The one exception was the workfare program in West Virginia, where the state's high unemployment and rural conditions severely limited job opportunities.

Table 2 (pages 24-27) compares the behavior over time of people in the "experimental" group (who were required to participate in the program) and people in the "control" group (who were not).[11] The results are for the primarily female AFDC group. As shown in the table, the program of mandatory job search followed by short-term workfare for AFDC applicants in San Diego increased the employment rate by 6 percentage points (from 55 percent to 61 percent) during the fifteen months of follow-up. Average total earnings during the same period—including the earnings of those who did not work as well as those who did—went up by $700 per person in the experimental group, representing a 23 percent increase over a control group member's average earnings. Roughly half of the gains in earnings came about because more women worked, and half because they obtained longer-lasting jobs or jobs with better pay or longer hours. The employment gains persisted, although at a somewhat reduced level, throughout the nearly eighteen months of follow-up.

In contrast, the program had minimal or no sustained employment effects on the primarily male group receiving AFDC-U assistance (not shown in Table 2).

As also indicated in Table 2, there were roughly similar employment gains in Arkansas, Maryland,[12] and Virginia, although the states varied dramatically in the subgroups of the AFDC rolls that they served and in the average earnings of the control groups.

The findings are quite different in West Virginia, where the relatively straightforward workfare program led to no increases in regular, unsubsidized employment. Although there are many possible explanations—including the design of the program or the characteristics of the women served—the most likely one—a weak state economy—was foreseen by the program's planners, who did not anticipate any employment gains. In a largely rural state with the nation's highest unemployment rate during part of the research period, a welfare employment initiative could provide a positive work experience without translating this into post-program unsubsidized employment gains.

West Virginia's program is a useful reminder that there are two sides to the labor market. Welfare employment programs focus on the supply side. In extreme cases, when the demand is not there, the provision of work experience and a change in the terms of the welfare "bargain" may simply not be enough to affect employment levels. Welfare recipients can be encouraged or required to take regular jobs, but the jobs must be available. The results to date suggest that demand constraints may be particularly acute in rural areas.[13]

The second positive finding is that the programs also led to some welfare savings although, compared to the effects on employment and earnings, the results were less consistent. In San Diego, over 18 months, average welfare payments per person in the experimental group were $288 below the average paid to members of the control group—a reduction in welfare outlays of almost 8 percent. Similar reductions occurred in Arkansas and Virginia but not in Baltimore and West Virginia. However, there was no evidence that, once people

## Table 2

Summary of the Impact of AFDC Work/Welfare Programs
in San Diego, Baltimore, Arkansas, Virginia, and West Virginia

| Outcome(a) | Experimentals | Controls | Difference | Decrease/Increase |
|---|---|---|---|---|
| *San Diego—Applicants* | | | | |
| Ever Employed | | | | |
| During 15 Months | 61.0% | 55.4% | +5.6%*** | +10% |
| Average Total Earnings | | | | |
| During 15 Months | $3802 | $3102 | +$700*** | +23% |
| Ever Received AFDC | | | | |
| Payments During 18 Months | 83.9% | 84.3% | −0.4% | 0% |
| Average Number of Months | | | | |
| Receiving AFDC Payments | | | | |
| During 18 Months | 8.13 | 8.61 | −0.48* | −6% |
| Average Total AFDC | | | | |
| Payments Received | | | | |
| During 18 Months | $3409 | $3697 | −$288** | −8% |
| *Baltimore—Applicants and Recipients* | | | | |
| Ever Employed | | | | |
| During 12 Months | 51.2% | 44.2% | +7.0%*** | +16% |

| | | | |
|---|---|---|---|
| Average Total Earnings During 12 Months | $1935 | $1759 | +$176 | +10% |
| Ever Received AFDC Payments During 15 Months | 94.9% | 95.1% | −0.2% | 0% |
| Average Number of Months Receiving AFDC Payments During 15 Months | 11.14 | 11.29 | −0.15 | −1% |
| Average Total AFDC Payments Received During 15 Months | $3058 | $3064 | −$6 | 0% |

*Arkansas—Applicants and Recipients*

| | | | | |
|---|---|---|---|---|
| Ever Employed During 6 Months | 18.8% | 14.0% | +4.8%** | +34% |
| Average Total Earnings During 6 Months | $291 | $213 | +$78* | +37% |
| Ever Received AFDC Payments During 9 Months | 72.8% | 75.9% | −3.1% | −4% |
| Average Number of Months Receiving AFDC Payments During 9 Months | 4.96 | 5.49 | −0.53*** | −10% |
| Average Total AFDC Payments Received During 9 Months | $772 | $865 | −$93*** | −11% |

**Table 2** (continued)

Summary of the Impact of AFDC Work/Welfare Programs
in San Diego, Baltimore, Arkansas, Virginia, and West Virginia

| Outcome(a) | Experimentals | Controls | Difference | Decrease/Increase |
|---|---|---|---|---|
| *Virginia—Applicants and Recipients* | | | | |
| Ever Employed | | | | |
| During 9 Months | 43.8% | 40.5% | +3.3%* | +8% |
| Average Total Earnings | | | | |
| During 9 Months | $1119 | $1038 | +$81 | +8% |
| Ever Received AFDC | | | | |
| Payments During 12 Months | 86.0% | 86.1% | −0.1% | 0% |
| Average Number of Months | | | | |
| Receiving AFDC Payments | | | | |
| During 12 Months | 7.75 | 7.90 | −0.14 | −2% |
| Average Total AFDC | | | | |
| Payments Received | | | | |
| During 12 Months | $1923 | $2007 | −$84** | −4% |
| *West Virginia—Applicants and Recipients* | | | | |
| Ever Employed | | | | |
| During 15 Months | 22.3% | 22.7% | −0.4% | −2% |
| Average Total Earnings | | | | |
| During 15 Months | $713 | $712 | $0 | 0% |

| | | | |
|---|---|---|---|
| Ever Received AFDC Payments During 21 Months | 96.8% | 96.0% | +0.8% | +1% |
| Average Number of Months Receiving AFDC Payments During 21 Months | 14.26 | 14.46 | −0.21 | −1% |
| Average Total AFDC Payments Received During 21 Months | $2681 | $2721 | −$40 | −1% |

*Source:* Final reports from programs in San Diego, Baltimore, Arkansas, Virginia, and West Virginia.

*Notes:* These data include zero values for sample members not employed and for sample members not receiving welfare payments. The estimates are regression-adjusted using ordinary least squares, controlling for pre-random assignment characteristics of sample members. There may be some discrepancies in calculating experimental-control differences due to rounding.

* Denotes statistical significance at the 10 percent level; ** at the 5 percent level; and *** at the 1 percent level.

(a) The length of follow-up varied by outcome and state. Employment and earnings were measured by calendar quarters. To assure that pre-program earnings were excluded from the impact estimates, the follow-up period began after the quarter of random assignment. In contrast, AFDC benefits were tracked for quarters beginning with the actual month of random assignment. As a result, the follow-up period for AFDC benefits was at least three months longer than that for employment and earnings.

had applied for welfare, they were deterred from completing the application process by the obligation to participate in a work program.

A third encouraging piece of information is that the programs were often most helpful for certain segments of the welfare caseload. For example, employment increases were usually greater for women receiving AFDC than for men in two-parent households (AFDC-U), and for those without prior employment compared to those with a recent work history. Although women and those without recent employment were still less likely to be working and more likely to be on welfare than their more advantaged counterparts, the employment requirements and services of the workfare programs helped narrow the gap.[14]

When benefits were compared to costs, results were generally positive. An examination of the programs' effects on the government budget shows that, not surprisingly, such initiatives cost money upfront, but, in general, the investment pays off in future savings in five years or less. In San Diego, an average dollar spent on the program for AFDC women led to estimated budget savings over a five-year period of over $2. Programs in Arkansas and Virginia also had estimated budget savings, but in Baltimore and West Virginia, there were some net costs.[15]

The research also offers some unusual findings about the distribution of benefits across federal, state, and county budgets, a question not often addressed in benefit-cost studies. In San Diego, where a detailed study was conducted, all three levels of government gained, based on the particular funding formula and matching arrangements that were in place. However, the federal government bore more than half of the costs and enjoyed the greatest net savings. Indeed, had there been no federal funds—or had there been substantially less federal funding—the state and county would have had no financial incentive to run these programs.[16] The findings highlight the importance of continued federal support to encourage states to undertake welfare employment initiatives that may ultimately prove cost-effective to operate.

Another way to look at program benefits and costs is to examine them from the perspectives of the groups targeted for participation—i.e., those who might have earned more as a result of the program, but who also might have lost money because of reductions in welfare and other transfer payments, such as Medicaid and Food Stamps. In most cases, the AFDC women came out ahead, the exceptions being in Arkansas, a state with very low grants, where almost any employment led to case closings; and West Virginia, where there were no gains in earnings. For men on AFDC-U, the story was very different. There were overall losses, not gains, from the programs, as reductions in welfare and other transfer payments exceeded increases in earnings.

What about the empty side of the glass? In what way do the results suggest caution? It is important to note that, although the programs produced changes, the magnitude of those changes was relatively modest. Across states, increases in quarterly employment rates were between 3 and 9 percentage points, excluding West Virginia where there were no employment gains. (Quarterly rates are not shown in Table 2.) Earnings in the four other states increased from $110 to $560 a year (including persons who did not find employment and had no earnings). Thus, while it is worthwhile to operate these programs, they will not move substantial numbers of people out of poverty.

### Issues and Lessons
Results to date from the work/welfare study suggest a number of major lessons.

*It is feasible, under certain conditions and on the scale at which the demonstration programs were implemented, to tie the receipt of welfare to participation obligations.* However, just as striking as the increases in participation these programs have achieved is the nature of the obligation. In most cases, it has been confined to job search, with workfare used only in a limited way for a relatively small number of people. This is due, in part, to funding constraints and to the sequencing of job search before work experience. It is also true that, when more funds have been available, states have often chosen to enrich the range of mandatory options rather than to impose a longer workfare requirement. The recent initiatives in California and Illinois include not only greater obligations but an expanded array of services beyond job search and workfare to such options as education, preparation for employment, and training.

*A number of quite different ways of structuring and targeting these programs will yield effective results.* Overall, the results do not point to a uniform program structure that merits national replication. Instead, one of the notable characteristics of these state welfare initiatives has been their diversity—in populations served, local conditions, and program design. A key explanation for the successful implementation of these initiatives may indeed be that states were given an opportunity to experiment and felt more ownership in the programs than they did in the earlier WIN Program, which was characterized by highly prescriptive central direction.

*In cases in which states chose to operate mandatory workfare, the interim results do not support the strongest claims of critics or advocates.* Despite critics' fears, workfare as implemented in the 1980s has been more often designed to provide useful work experience than simply to enforce a *quid pro quo*—although both objectives may be present. As a result, the work positions quite often resemble quality public service employment jobs, structured to meet public needs and to provide meaningful work experience. Under these conditions—when the jobs are considered worthwhile and the obligation is limited, as it is in most states—welfare recipients generally do not object to working for their grants.

On the other hand, the interim findings do not support the more extreme claims of proponents. The work positions developed few new skills. Although the San Diego findings provide some evidence that adding workfare after job search may increase a program's effectiveness, the West Virginia results are a cautious reminder that, at least in certain conditions, what is needed is not only workfare positions but regular jobs.[17] Furthermore, there was no evidence in San Diego that the work mandate, as it was administered, deterred individuals from completing their welfare applications or "smoked out" large numbers of AFDC women who held jobs with unreported income.

Thus, arguments for and against workfare—and participation obligations more broadly defined—may involve not so much a choice between those who want to reduce welfare costs and those who fear that the programs are coercive as an opportunity to change the values, politics, and perceived fairness of the welfare system. These issues remain prominent in state debates on policy options, in which questions of values are often as central as questions about likely savings. Some argue—as did the West Virginia welfare commissioner in 1982—that even if workfare costs more to begin with, its design is preferable because it fits with the nation's values and improves the image of welfare. In contrast, others continue to emphasize that what is needed is not requirements but jobs, as well as investments in training, education, and child care that will help people find the kinds of work that confer economic security in the long run.

*The programs led to relatively modest increases in employment, which in some cases translated into even smaller welfare savings. Nonetheless, the changes were usually large enough to justify the programs' costs, although this finding varied by state and target group.* For those accustomed to grandiose claims for social programs, the outcomes for these initiatives—as well as for other welfare employment programs—may look small. With gains that are not dramatic and only limited savings, the programs do not offer a cure for poverty or a short-cut to balancing the budget. This may prompt critics to reject these approaches, claiming that 3 to 9 percentage point gains in employment or 8 to 37 percent increases in earnings are unsatisfactory. There are, however, several reasons to conclude otherwise.

First, there is always a strong temptation to search for a simple solution to a complex problem. The welfare debate is filled with this kind of rhetoric. Now, faced with the reality of limited gains, it may be tempting to seek another "solution," for which there is no similar evidence. Yet, given the fact that reliable findings on the effects of social policies are rare, the striking feature of these programs is their consistently positive outcomes in a wide range of environments, with the sole exception of the very unusual circumstances in West Virginia. There is no comparable evidence on an alternative strategy.

Second, since the study measured changes for samples that were representative of large groups in the welfare caseload, results in the range of 5 percentage points take on added importance. The outcomes are also expressed as averages for a wide range of individuals, some of whom gained little or nothing from the program (including those who never received any services) and others who gained more. Thus, even relatively small changes, multiplied by large numbers of people, have considerable policy significance.

Third, the lessons from the demonstration suggest ways to make these programs more effective and provide evidence that some groups—for example, those without recent work histories—benefit more substantially than others.[18] Fourth, it is possible that the short-term effects may underestimate the longer-term gains, especially if attitudes toward AFDC shift as the concept of reciprocal obligations becomes more accepted. (On the other hand, there is evidence that, in some cases, effects that are initially positive may decay over time.)

Finally, the benefit-cost findings suggest that, within a relatively short time, program savings often offset costs, a balance that represents about as much as any social program has been able to achieve. While previous smaller-scale tests of special programs have produced cost-effective results, this study provides the first solid evidence of such outcomes in a major ongoing service delivery system. The ability to effect change on a large scale is an important new achievement.

# Unanswered Questions

Although these state initiatives provide a wealth of information about the implementation and effectiveness of alternative approaches to reforming welfare with work, they leave unanswered a number of questions about the design and scale of programs.

The results summarized in this paper are for programs that have participation obligations of limited intensity, cost, or duration. They primarily required job search and short-term work experience. One unanswered question is whether more costly, comprehensive programs— providing either more services or longer obligations—would have greater effects.

Several states are using or plan to provide more intensive services or requirements, including educational remediation and training, and to complement these with extensive child-care services. Two examples are the Greater Avenues for Independence (GAIN) legislation in California and the Employment and Training (ET) Choices program in Massachusetts. Another more intensive approach is Supported Work, a program offering paid transitional work experience under conditions of close supervision, peer support, and generally increasing responsibilities.[19] Supported Work was tested as a voluntary program and found effective for women with histories of long-term welfare dependency. Although the incremental return to larger investments is not clear, the persistence of dependency for many, even after job search or short-term workfare, provides a rationale for states to offer more intensive services, while evaluating them to see whether they lead to long-term rewards.

A second open question concerns the broader implications of an ongoing participation requirement on family formation, the well-being of children, and attitudes toward work. It is important to note that child care was not a major issue in these programs, since their requirements were mostly short-term and limited mainly to women with school-age children. However, the availability and quality of child care would be much more important if either of these conditions changed, or if the programs made even larger differences in the rate at which women moved out of the home and into permanent jobs.

A third unanswered question is whether relatively low-cost mandatory programs will prove effective for the most disadvantaged groups of welfare recipients, those facing major barriers to employment (e.g., those with substantial language problems or educational deficiencies). Although there is evidence that the programs have a stronger impact on recipients who have some obstacles to employment—as opposed to the more job-ready who will find employment on their own —additional study is required to determine whether there is a threshold below which more intensive assistance is needed.[20]

A fourth unanswered question concerns the feasibility of operating larger-scale universal programs, and whether they would have the same results. The pre-1980 work mandates often foundered on legal, political, and bureaucratic obstacles, but the more recent large-scale initiatives in the MDRC study were implemented more smoothly.[21] It is not clear, however, whether work programs can be extended to an even greater share of the AFDC caseload (including the majority of AFDC women with younger children) without compromising quality, encountering political or administrative resistance, or raising broader issues such as whether welfare recipients would displace regular workers either during or after the program.[22]

Also, as the West Virginia findings suggest, in rural areas with very weak economic conditions, workfare serves as a jobs program, not as a transition to unsubsidized employment. A major unanswered question is the more precise relationship between the effectiveness of the programs and economic conditions, and whether this relationship is affected by the scale of the program.

In addition, all of the results were measured only over the short term. Whether these results persist, increase, or decay is important in judging the potential of the work/welfare approach.

Finally, while there is substantial information on the effectiveness of these programs, it remains unclear whether the achievements come from the services provided or from the mandatory aspect of the programs.[23] Although the distinction between mandatory and voluntary programs is sometimes not as great as one might think—since most nominally mandatory programs seek voluntary compliance and involvement—some differences exist and their importance remains uncertain.

# General Conclusions About Work/Welfare Programs

$\mathbf{A}$t the outset, this paper outlined the multiple goals of welfare policy and the continuing search for a balance that might more successfully provide income without distorting incentives for work or family formation. MDRC's five-year experiment testing limited work requirements has provided some new evidence to inform this debate. As expected, the lessons are complex.

The continuing interest in work solutions, even in states with very weak labor markets, is testimony to the important political and value issues inherent in the debate. Issues of equity, concerns about a system that may send the wrong signals or encourage long-term dependency, the stigma associated with public assistance, and the widespread unpopularity of the welfare system—all of these have pushed states to add some type of an obligation to AFDC. However, the interest in such programs continues to be tempered by funding constraints and an understandable unwillingness to set up ones that stress obligations at the expense of providing opportunities that help people move off the rolls or of assuring the well-being of children.

The results of recent research suggest that introducing a stronger work emphasis into the AFDC program ultimately will not cost but save money—although it will cost money in the short run. Thus, the claims of both critics and advocates described earlier contain a measure of truth. In the past, social programs have been oversold and then discredited when they failed to cure problems. In contrast these findings provide a timely warning that welfare employment initiatives will not be a panacea but can provide meaningful improvement. The extent of the changes, however, suggests that the major arguments may continue to center around politics and values as well as the different ways to increase the programs' effectiveness.

The modest nature of the improvements also indicates that welfare employment obligations can be only part of a "solution" to poverty. Other reforms—for example, changes in the tax laws and expansion of the earned income tax credit to increase the rewards for work, educational reforms, training and retraining, increased child-support enforcement, and job-creation programs—are important complements if welfare is not only to be made more politically acceptable but also to succeed in reducing poverty substantially.

The fact that there is support for work programs—within the general public and the welfare population—argues for a welfare reform approach that promotes and also rewards work. Workfare, narrowly defined, does the former, but to the extent that it does not deter dependency or assist many people off the welfare rolls, it may not provide enough added income and adequately combat dependency. What this suggests is that there be both requirements within the welfare system and added opportunities and rewards for leaving welfare. "Sticks" may be a part of the solution, but "carrots" are also merited if work is to be more an alternative to than a punishment for being poor.

# Notes

1. The research for the study of state work/welfare initiatives has been supported by the Ford, Winthrop Rockefeller, and Claude Worthington Benedum foundations, the Congressional Research Service of the Library of Congress, and the states of Arizona, Arkansas, California, Florida, Illinois, Maine, Maryland, New Jersey, Texas, Virginia, and West Virginia. The research and the conclusions reached by the author, however, do not necessarily reflect the official positions of the funders.

2. The author wishes to acknowledge with gratitude the helpful comments made on an earlier draft of this paper by Gordon Berlin of the Ford Foundation and Robert Reischauer of the Brookings Institution, as well as those made by members of MDRC staff, including Michael Bangser, Daniel Friedlander, Barbara Goldman, and James Riccio.

3. That is, the findings showed that the impact of changing the AFDC income floor and tax rate for persons currently eligible was relatively small, but the impact on the number eligible for assistance was large. As a result, work reductions—which were modest for the current caseload—could become larger when combined with the work reductions of persons newly eligible. Moreover, a substantial share of the additional cost of extending AFDC to two-parent households would simply go toward replacing reduced earnings rather than raising income.

39

4. Both plans are sometimes called two-track approaches, since AFDC recipients would be divided into those required to work (e.g., women with children six years and over) and those not expected to work (e.g., women with responsibilities for young children).

5. See, for example, the discussion in Gould-Stuart, 1982.

6. For a more detailed discussion of the design of the study and the interim findings, see Gueron, 1986.

7. In Table 1, "AFDC" refers to welfare cases that are usually headed by a single parent, usually a woman; "AFDC-U" refers to cases headed by two parents (with the principal earner unemployed) and where the targeted participant is usually male. All AFDC-U case heads are required to register with the WIN program (i.e., are "WIN-mandatory") as are most AFDC case heads with children at least six years of age. "Applicants" are individuals who were studied from the time at which they applied for welfare, and some of whom subsequently became welfare recipients (but continue to be called applicants in this study). "Recipients" are individuals who were receiving welfare benefits when the study began. (In some states, the study was limited to those recipients who had just become WIN-mandatory; in other cases the program covered the full range of recipients.)

8. The final reports now available are: Friedlander et al., 1985a; Friedlander et al., 1985b; Friedlander et al., 1986b; Goldman et al., 1986; and Riccio et al., 1986. Interim findings from the studies are included in the following reports: Auspos, 1985; Ball, 1984; Goldman et al., 1984; Goldman et al., 1985; MDRC, 1985; Price, 1985; Quint, 1984a; Quint, 1984b; Quint and Guy, 1986. In a number of these states, data are currently being collected that will extend the follow-up for a longer period of time.

9. The same survey was recently conducted with participants and supervisors in New York City's workfare program. Although in general the results were similar to those in the other six states, it appears that participants in New York City, Chicago, and Baltimore shared less favorable views about

mandatory work obligations than those in the other areas. Nevertheless, the majority of participants in these cities perceived these obligations as being fair. See Hoerz and Hanson, 1986, p. 32.

10. Bane and Ellwood, 1983; and Ellwood, 1986.

11. People were assigned to the experimental or control groups when they applied for welfare, were required to register with the WIN program, or had their WIN status reviewed. As discussed above, not all experimentals actually participated in program activities or (if they were new applicants) received welfare payments. In addition, although controls could not receive special program services, they were eligible for other employment and training services in the community and sometimes for regular WIN services. For a further explanation of cross-state differences in sample composition, control services, or experimental participation patterns, see the detailed final reports on each state.

12. In Maryland, the length of follow-up was notably short, given the longer duration of program services for some participants. To ensure that the study did not mistake the program's accomplishments, additional work is now under way to determine whether the measured impacts increase or decay over a longer period.

13. The Virginia and Arkansas studies also showed lower or no employment gains in rural, as compared to urban areas. See Riccio et al., 1986; and Friedlander et al., 1985a.

14. A preliminary study suggests that this pattern of differences is not as clear for long-term recipients. See Friedlander and Long, 1987.

15. As indicated in footnote 12, the Baltimore results may change when data covering a longer follow-up period become available.

16. For San Diego the benefit-cost analysis showed that the benefits to the state and county exceeded their costs by $314 per experimental. For the federal government the comparable net benefit was $676 per experimental. Total costs were estimated at $636 per experimental, of which the federal

government paid $443, or 70 percent, and the state and county paid $193, or 30 percent. If most of the federal costs had been shifted to the state and county, their overall costs would have exceeded their share of program benefits, eliminating any incentive to operate the program. See Goldman et al., 1986 and unpublished data.

17. One unusual feature of the San Diego study was the simultaneous random assignment of AFDC applicants to a control group and to two experimental treatments: job search alone and job search followed by short-term workfare. The results showed that job search alone also had positive impacts (i.e., employment gains and welfare savings), but the findings were less consistent and the gains in earnings smaller than for the combined program.

This suggests that, under certain circumstances, employment impacts may be greater if individuals who do not find employment in job-search workshops are required to meet a short-term work obligation. For further discussion of the findings for the programs in San Diego and West Virginia, see Goldman et al., 1986; and Friedlander et al., 1986b.

18. In addition, data on changes in the distribution of income provide some tentative information on possible ways to improve such programs in the future. For example, the Baltimore initiative (a relatively more intensive program with not only job search, but also work experience, education, and training) was more likely to move some individuals into higher categories of earnings (i.e., earnings above a full-time, minimum-wage job) than the Arkansas program (a very low-cost version of job search).

Other results suggest that the level of welfare grants is also important, since in states with high grants, employment increases more often resulted in net gains in total income (i.e., earnings plus welfare payments). See Friedlander, et al., 1985b; Friedlander et al., 1985a; and Goldman et al., 1986.

19. MDRC, 1980.

20. See Friedlander and Long, 1987.

21. See Gueron and Nathan, 1985, for a summary of this earlier experience.

22. A study of another type of job guarantee—paid work experience for youths as opposed to unpaid workfare for welfare recipients—suggested a possible trade-off between job quality and displacement. See Ball et al., 1981.

23. Other studies, not reported in this paper, show that voluntary job-search and work-experience programs also are effective for AFDC women. See Manpower Demonstration Research Corporation, 1980, and Wolfhagen, 1983.

# References

Auspos, Patricia; with Ball, Joseph; Goldman, Barbara; and Gueron, Judith. 1985. *Maine: Interim Findings From a Grant Diversion Program*. New York: Manpower Demonstration Research Corporation.

Ball, Joseph; and Wolfhagen, Carl; with Gerould, David; and Solnick, Loren. 1981. *The Participation of Private Businesses as Work Sponsors in the Youth Entitlement Demonstration*. New York: Manpower Demonstration Research Corporation.

Ball, Joseph; with Hamilton, Gayle; Hoerz, Gregory; Goldman, Barbara; and Gueron, Judith. 1984. *West Virginia: Interim Findings on the Community Work Experience Demonstrations*. New York: Manpower Demonstration Research Corporation.

Bane, Mary Jo; and Ellwood, David T. 1983. *The Dynamics of Dependence: The Routes to Self-Sufficiency*. Cambridge, Mass.: Urban Systems Research and Engineering, Inc.

Ellwood, David T. 1986. *Targeting "Would-Be" Long-Term Recipients of AFDC*. Princeton, New Jersey: Mathematica Policy Research, Inc.

Friedlander, Daniel; Hoerz, Gregory; Quint, Janet; Riccio, James; with Goldman, Barbara; Gueron, Judith; and Long, David. 1985a. *Arkansas: Final Report on the WORK Program in Two Counties*. New York: Manpower Demonstration Research Corporation.

Friedlander, Daniel; Hoerz, Gregory; Long, David; Quint, Janet; with Goldman, Barbara; and Gueron, Judith. 1985b. *Maryland: Final Report on the Employment Initiatives Evaluation.* New York: Manpower Demonstration Research Corporation.

Friedlander, Daniel; Goldman, Barbara; Gueron, Judith; and Long, David. 1986a. "Initial Findings From the Demonstration of State Work/Welfare Initiatives," *The American Economic Review* 76: pp. 224-229.

Friedlander, Daniel; Erickson, Marjorie; Hamilton, Gayle; Knox, Virginia; with Goldman, Barbara; Gueron, Judith; and Long, David. 1986b. *West Virginia: Final Report on the Community Work Experience Demonstrations.* New York: Manpower Demonstration Research Corporation.

Friedlander, Daniel; and Long, David. 1987. "A Study of Performance Measures and Subgroup Impacts in Three Welfare Employment Programs." New York: Manpower Demonstration Research Corporation.

Goldman, Barbara; Gueron, Judith; Ball, Joseph; Price, Marilyn; with Friedlander, Daniel; and Hamilton, Gayle. 1984. *Preliminary Findings From the San Diego Job Search and Work Experience Demonstration.* New York: Manpower Demonstration Research Corporation.

Goldman, Barbara; Friedlander, Daniel; Gueron, Judith; Long, David; with Hamilton, Gayle; and Hoerz, Gregory. 1985. *Findings From the San Diego Job Search and Work Experience Demonstration.* New York: Manpower Demonstration Research Corporation.

Goldman, Barbara; Friedlander, Daniel; Long, David; with Erickson, Marjorie; and Gueron, Judith. 1986. *Final Report on the San Diego Job Search and Work Experience Demonstration.* New York: Manpower Demonstration Research Corporation.

Gould-Stuart, Joanna, 1982. *Welfare Women in A Group Job Search Program: Their Experiences in the Louisville WIN Research Laboratory Project.* New York: Manpower Demonstration Research Corporation.

Gueron, Judith M. 1986. *Work Initiatives For Welfare Recipients: Lessons From a Multi-State Experiment.* New York: Manpower Demonstration Research Corporation.

Gueron, Judith. 1985. "The Demonstration of State Work/Welfare Initiatives." *Randomization and Field Experimentation: New Directions for Program Evaluation,* No. 28, pp. 5-13.

Gueron, Judith; and Nathan, Richard. 1985. "The MDRC Work/Welfare Project: Objectives, Status, Significance." *Policy Studies Review* 4: pp. 417-432.

Hoerz, Gregory; and Hanson, Karla. 1986. "A Survey of Participants and Worksite Supervisors in the New York City Work Experience Program." New York: Manpower Demonstration Research Corporation.

Manpower Demonstration Research Corporation. 1985. *Baseline Paper on the Evaluation of the WIN Demonstration Program in Cook County, Illinois.* New York: Manpower Demonstration Research Corporation.

Manpower Demonstration Research Corporation. 1980. *Summary and Findings of the National Supported Work Demonstration.* Cambridge, Mass.: Ballinger Publishing Co.

Price, Marilyn; with Ball, Joseph; Goldman, Barbara; Gruber, David; Gueron, Judith; and Hamilton, Gayle. 1985. *Interim Findings From the Virginia Employment Services Program.* New York: Manpower Demonstration Research Corporation.

Quint, Janet; with Goldman, Barbara; and Gueron, Judith. 1984a. *Interim Findings From the Arkansas WIN Demonstration Program.* New York: Manpower Demonstration Research Corporation.

Quint, Janet; with Ball, Joseph; Goldman, Barbara; Gueron, Judith; and Hamilton, Gayle. 1984b. *Interim Findings From the Maryland Employment Initiatives Programs.* New York: Manpower Demonstration Research Corporation.

Quint, Janet; Guy, Cynthia; with Hoerz, Gregory; Hamilton, Gayle; Ball, Joseph; Goldman, Barbara; and Gueron, Judith. 1986. *Interim Findings From the Illinois WIN*

*Demonstration Program in Cook County.* New York: Manpower Demonstration Research Corporation.

Riccio, James; Cave, George; Freedman, Stephen; Price, Marilyn; with Friedlander, Daniel; Goldman, Barbara; Gueron, Judith; and Long, David. 1986. *Final Report on the Virginia Employment Services Program.* New York: Manpower Demonstration Research Corporation.

Wolfhagen, Carl; with Goldman, Barbara. 1983. *Job Search Strategies: Lessons from the Louisville WIN Laboratory Project.* New York: Manpower Demonstration Research Corporation.

Judith M. Gueron is president of the Manpower Demonstration Research Corporation (MDRC), a nonprofit organization that designs, manages, and studies demonstration projects aimed at increasing the self-sufficiency of economically disadvantaged groups, including long-term welfare recipients, school dropouts, and teenage parents. Dr. Gueron has directed numerous large-scale national studies and is the principal investigator of the Demonstration of Work/Welfare Initiatives, a multi-state evaluation of welfare employment programs. She received a Ph.D. in economics from Harvard University and has published extensively in the field of welfare and employment.